Pucks, Clubs, and Baseball Gloves

Reading and Writing **Sports Poems**

compiled and annotated by Jill Kalz

PICTURE WINDOW BOOKS
a capstone imprint

Special thanks to our adviser for his expertise:

Terry Flaherty, PhD, Professor of English
Minnesota State University, Mankato

Editor: Jill Kalz
Designer: Lori Bye
Art Director: Nathan Gassman
Production Specialist: Kathy McColley

Illustration Credits
Cristian Bernardini, cover, 4, 5, 7, 10, 22, 24, 28, 29, 32; Dustin Burkes-Larrañaga, 1, 6, 8, 21; Sandra D'Antonio, 14, 19, 31;
Matt Loveridge, back cover, 2-3, 9, 12-13, 17, 18, 23; Simon Smith, 11, 15, 26-27; Tou Yia Xiong, 16, 20, 25

Picture Window Books are published by Capstone,
1710 Roe Crest Drive, North Mankato, Minnesota 56003
www.capstonepub.com

Library of Congress Cataloging-in-Publication Data
Cataloging-in-publication information is on file with the Library of Congress.
ISBN 978-1-4795-2196-8 (library binding)
ISBN 978-1-4795-2947-6 (paperback)
ISBN 978-1-4795-3330-5 (eBook PDF)

Printed in the United States of America in Brainerd, Minnesota.
092013   007770BANGS14

TABLE OF CONTENTS

DISCOVER THE POET IN YOU

Sports are a big part of people's lives all around the world. Not only are they a good source of exercise, sports teach us valuable lessons: how to get along with others, how to be a good loser, how to set goals and go beyond them. What's your favorite sport to watch or play? Celebrate it by writing a poem. Share how a tennis ball, hockey puck, or football feels in your hand. Share how the cars roar around the track, how your skis "shush" in the snow.

WHY WRITE POETRY?

When you write poetry, you're an explorer. You discover new words, new combinations of words, and new meanings. You use old words in fresh ways. Poetry opens your ears. Sentences can play like music. Poetry opens your eyes. It's as if you're seeing the world around you—your ordinary, everyday world—for the very first time. Poetry can be a new language that allows you to share your ideas and experiences.

WHAT TOOLS DOES A POET USE?

Whether you're building a house, a car, or a video game, you need tools to get the job done. Poets use tools to build their poems too. Their tools include parts of speech (such as nouns, verbs, and adjectives), ways of writing (like different forms or types of poetry), and the cool sounds that letters and words make when they're combined (like rhymes and repeated letters). Knowing what the tools are and how to use them is what this book is all about.

HOW DO I READ THIS BOOK?

Start by reading the poems. All of them are about sports. After you read each one, take a look at the Info Box on the bottom of the page. There you'll find definitions of poetic forms and tools. You may also find helpful tips, questions to consider, or writing prompts. Near the back of the book, you'll have the chance to review what you've learned and practice writing your own poems. Before you know it, you'll be a poet!

A Hole in One

The putting green is in my sight.
My hat is on—the sun is bright!
A hole in one would please me. See,
I rest the ball on the tiny tee.
I choose my club—it fits just right.
I close my fingers, squeeze it tight.
I aim. The hole, it looks so small.
Back, then forward—hit the ball!
It zips! It zings! That ball is fast!
But wait ... it misses, whizzes past.
And sadly, in the lake right there,
My ball goes PLUNK! It isn't fair!
One hole down, 17 in sight,
My hole in one might take till night.

—Catherine Ipcizade

SOUNDS LIKE ...

When words end in the same sound, they **rhyme**. In the poem above, "sight" and "bright" rhyme. So do "see" and "tee," and "right" and "tight." Rhyming words can add interest and structure to a poem. What other rhymes can you find in this poem?

There Once Was a Girl Who Could Kick ...

There once was a girl who could kick,
spent all of her days kicking sticks,
till she spotted a ball,
kicked it clear through a wall,
and began playing soccer right quick.

—Catherine Ipcizade

A **limerick** is a silly five-line poem. The first, second, and last lines rhyme ("kick / sticks / quick"). The third and fourth lines are shorter and rhyme with each other ("ball / wall"). Try writing a limerick about a boy who could jump or throw.

Cross-Country Runners

Striding, legs churning,
racing cross the field.
Surging, lungs burning,
sprinting to the woods.

Now hurtling down a packed-dirt path,
passing proud parents
and two startled deer.

Arms pumping, feet thumping,
they are blood and muscle,
air and bone.

Hearts hammering,
caught up in the chase.
Running for the love
of running.

—Mark Weakland

STICKING TOGETHER

A **stanza** is a group of lines that is usually separated by a blank line, called a **stanza break**. Stanzas often contain complete thoughts or images. Stanza breaks cue the reader to pause and let the words linger, before moving on to the rest of the poem.

Baseball

Bats crack as they collide with the ball.
Athletes sprint as they strive to give all.
Spectators cheer to "pick up the pace,"
Eager to urge runners round the base.
Bases all touched as he sprints to home plate.
A catcher, determined to change the game's fate!
Look to the crowd as they scream out his name,
Love for the team, and a love for the game!

— Matt Loveridge

HIDE AND SEEK

An **acrostic** is a poem with a secret. When the first letter of each line is put together, it spells another word or phrase. Sometimes that hidden message is the poem's main idea or title of the poem. Try writing an acrostic about your favorite sports team.

Old Manny

Old Manny the meerkat could run.
He ran in the rain and the sun.
He jumped over hurdles,
laughed at the turtles,
and raced all the jackals for fun.

—Catherine Ipcizade

CAN YOU FEEL IT?

Rhythm is the "drum" in poetry. It can be created by **beats** or **syllables**. You can measure rhythm in **meter**—just count the beats or stressed syllables in each line. Read aloud, and tap the beats with your finger: "Old MAN-ny the MEER-kat could RUN ..."

Hail Mary Pass

receiver
tall, lanky
spinning, dodging, sprinting
yards, end zone, quarterback, throw
leaping, flying, catching
excited, triumphant
touchdown

—Blake Hoena

WHAT A GEM

The diamond-shaped **diamante** uses a parts-of-speech pattern. The seven-line poem starts with a noun. Two adjectives and three verbs follow. Next come four nouns, three verbs, and two adjectives. The final noun is often the opposite of the first.

Ode to Quarterback Joe

Listen my children, and I'll tell you a story
of Quarterback Joe, who dreamed of great glory.

Near the end of the game, when the score was a tie,
Joe took to the field with a glint in his eye.

He huddled his teammates and described his game plan,
"I'll hand off to Bob. He'll run fast as he can.

"And after that play, Bob will run it some more.
Then I'll pass it to Jay, and we'll win when we score!"

The guys cheered and clapped then got ready to strike.
Joe called the cadence, "Twenty-one, down, set, *hike*!"

But the running back tripped. He stumbled then fell.
So Joe had to scramble, and as he scrambled, he yelled,

TELL ME A STORY

Narrative poems tell stories. Other than that, there aren't any rules. They may be long or short, rhyming or not. The stories may be simple or complex. They may include action and **dialogue**. What details does this poet use to keep you interested in the story?

"Receivers! Go deep! Run, run like the wind!
I'll throw a long bomb!" And that's when Joe grinned.

For Joe knew his arm was the best in the nation.
He could pinpoint receivers in far-off locations.

Because of Joe's talent, the defense was toast,
so he heaved a great pass toward the end zone's goalpost.

The ball was a rocket. It punctured a cloud
and just missed a plane. "Holy cow!" cried the crowd.

Then down the ball hurtled, the crowd leaped to its feet,
and Quarterback Joe cried, "The other team's beat!"

Joe's receiver leaped up, hands poised for reception,
        but then ...
"*Oh no!*" groaned the crowd. "It's a dang *interception*!"

Mark Weakland

Swish

Inhale ... Ball echoes
on the cold, scratched, worn gym floor.
He takes the shot ... Breathe ...

—Catherine Ipcizade

DO YOU HAIKU?

A **haiku** is a Japanese form of poetry. It has three lines and follows a 5-7-5 pattern of syllables. Lines 1 and 3 have five syllables. Line 2 has seven. The poem above is short, but it tells us a lot. What do we learn about the player? About where he's playing?

Around and Around and Around

"Drivers, start your engines!"
The green flag waves, and the race is on!
In a haze of fumes and a thunderous growl,
Around and around and around they go.

Blazing metal and lightning speed.
Helmeted drivers with nerves of steel.
There's the smell of rubber as they bank the curves.
Around and around and around they go.

One-hundred fifty miles an hour.
Sometimes 200 and a little more!
Hurtling past in a deafening roar,
Around and around and around they go.

Zooming through the final laps,
Number 3 is in the lead.
But 2 and 12 are right behind!
And the winner is, at the checkered flag ... Number 3!
Around and around and around they go.

—Mark Weakland

AGAIN AND AGAIN

When poets use **repetition**, they repeat certain words, phrases, or sounds. Repetition can help create patterns. It can also help make a point. Every stanza in this poem ends with the same phrase. What effect does this repeated phrase have?

Hockey

Blades flash.
Sticks smash and slash.
Puck, hard and black, zooming.
Skaters racing, checking, shooting.
Action!

—Mark Weakland

HIGH FIVE

A **cinquain** (sin-CANE) is a five-line poem. "Cinq" means "five" in French. The poem follows a 2-4-6-8-2 pattern of syllables.

Count the syllables in the poem above with your fingers. Feel the pattern? Try writing a cinquain about your favorite sport.

Destination

I am a horse, a noble steed.
Thus I was born to run.

I do it for my rider,
not merely idle fun.

My rider has a need to get
quickly to his goal.

This is what I've trained for,
ever since I was a foal.

We work together as a team
to beat the slower herd.

I stretch my legs to take the lead
when I hear him give the word.

We must be getting near the place.
He's made me run so fast.

I hope that there's a feedbag
or a field of soft green grass.

When finally we reach our goal,
I find myself down-hearted.

After all the blood and sweat and tears,
we're right back where we started.

—Matt Loveridge

QUITE A PAIR

A pair of poetry lines is called a **couplet**. The lines usually rhyme, but, as shown above, they don't have to. A couplet often stands as a unit, making its own image or point. What is the main image of each couplet in this poem?

Learning to Ski

Butterflies in my stomach seem to carry me up the mountain. I reach the end of my rope just as I reach the top of the mountain. I have conquered the bunny hill! First I face the slope as it stares me down.

Then I face my fears and attack the slope. My fears are left at the top of the mountain.

—Matt Loveridge

PICTURE POEM

Concrete poems look like their subjects. See how the words in the poem above talk about a ski slope and look like a ski slope too? Try writing a concrete poem about a baseball or ice skate. How about a curling ocean wave, perfect for surfing?

Animal Games

There once was a hippo named Rocky
Whose favorite sport was hockey
He played goalie but always got stuck
In the net when he blocked a puck

Belinda the Yak, she liked to play
Tennis with her herd every day
Because the court was covered in grass
They always had plenty of tasty snacks

Katie the Snake hoped to play basketball
But she was more long than she was tall
And Steven the Zebra played Frisbee
With his friend Carl the Chimpanzee

Ollie the Ostrich was a skateboarder
And Henry the Hyena a figure skater
George the Rhino played soccer
While Larry the Giraffe was a boxer

But when it came time to play one sport
The group would bellow, argue, and snort
Until Marie the Lioness giggled and sprang
After them all for a game of tag

—Blake Hoena

COUNT TO FOUR

A stanza with four lines is called a **quatrain**. The poem above is made of rhyming quatrains that follow an AABB pattern. The ends of the first and second lines rhyme ("Rocky / hockey"). So do the third and fourth lines ("stuck / puck").

Ping-Pong

Ping-Pong.

Back and forth.

I have a paddle.

A net's in the middle.

You hit it to me.

What could be easier?

Long ago

Now table tennis is

Whiff-whaff,

You hit it to me.

I love this sport!

Ping-Pong!

So do you.

Ping-Pong!

I hit it to you.

Ping-Pong!

it was called "flim-flam."

Ping-Pong!

I love this game!

Ping ... Oops!

—Mark Weakland

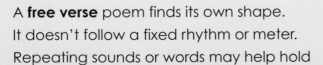
FREE TO BE

A **free verse** poem finds its own shape. It doesn't follow a fixed rhythm or meter. Repeating sounds or words may help hold the poem together. Here the repetition of the word "Ping-Pong" creates a fun echo, like a ball being batted back and forth.

Like a Shark Attack!

Backstroke,
freestyle,
floating on my back,
I swim in laps,
I circle quick,
like a shark attack!
Jumping high
then diving low,
imagine sea life
down below.
My snorkel on,
my goggles snug,
I drift along—
a floating slug.

—Catherine Ipcizade

MAKING PICTURES

Imagery is what you picture in your mind when you read a poem. Details like colors, sounds, textures, smells, and flavors all help create imagery. In this poem, the poet uses a **simile**. She compares the circling swimmer to a shark ("*like* a shark attack").

Barnyard Soccer

Two teams line up, the Tupelo Turtles
against the Mighty Minceville Mudhens,
to play soccer on Farmer Susie's estate.
They use the front yard for a field
while one goal is a gaping wooden gate,
and the other, a hole in the hen house.
The ball is a bound-up bag of barley and oats.

To start, Kirby the Turtle kicks the ball to Kurt
the Alpaca who passes it to Pamela the Pig.
Then Henry the Horse sticks his hoof out
to steal the ball and boots it down to Barney
the Goat who scores the game's first goal.
Ten hours later, it's tied 20-20,
and they'd probably still be playing if Pete
the Ox didn't break open the bag of oats
and barley because he needed a snack.

—Blake Hoena

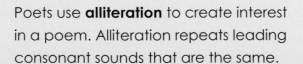

22

Poets use **alliteration** to create interest in a poem. Alliteration repeats leading consonant sounds that are the same.

In the poem above, "Tupelo Turtles" and "bound-up bag of barley" are examples of alliteration. Can you find four more?

The Pole-Vaulter

Here I come.
I'm running fast!
A galloping unicorn with a 10-foot horn.

I plant the pole.
I give a leap!
A quivering spring, the pole flings me skyward.

Whoosh! I'm a rocket.
Wahoo! I'm a bird!
I spread my wings and sail over the bar.

And now I'm falling.
Falling down, down, down,
until I—THUD!—hit the mat.

With a bounce I'm done,
back to Earth. That was fun!
I want to do it again!

—Mark Weakland

WHAT IT IS

Poets often use **metaphors** to compare one thing to another. A metaphor tries to show that two things have something in common. In the poem above, "unicorn" is a metaphor for the speaker. The girl is running (galloping) with a long pole (a unicorn horn).

Hugo the Skateboarding Dog

My bulldog Hugo has liked to carve up
the pavement on his purple penny board
since he was just an itty-bitty pup.
Now, whenever he gets a little bored

Hugo jumps on his deck and bombs down hills
swerving to the left and then to the right.
If you saw him, you'd say he had mad skills
as he cruised down the street and out of sight.

Sometimes, Hugo just wants to catch some air.
He'll skate up to a rail and then Ollie
kickflipping to a grind with doggy flair.
He hits a trick and gets all slobbery

happily wagging the nub of his tail.
Yeah, he's no newb, hitting tricks without fail.

—Blake Hoena

SEE A PATTERN?

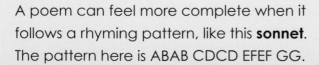

A poem can feel more complete when it follows a rhyming pattern, like this **sonnet**. The pattern here is ABAB CDCD EFEF GG.

The ends of lines 1 and 3 rhyme ("A"). So do lines 2 and 4 ("B"). Which words in the poem do "C," "D," "E," "F," and "G" represent?

Ode to a Soccer Game

O game of passes, heads, and kicks,
"action" is your middle name!
With sprints and leaps and dribbling tricks,
you put the other sports to shame.

How lovely is your soccer ball!
A perfect sphere, so firm and round.
With leather panels (32 in all)
it skips and bounces cross the ground.

Here comes that ball! It whacks my chest
and knocks the wind right out of me.
But I keep running. There is no rest.
I kick and hit ... the referee!

Down the field I huff and snort,
run and jump, then lose control.
O soccer, you'd be my favorite sport,
if I could only make a goal!

—Mark Weakland

WHAT A FEELING!

An **ode** is a type of **lyric poem**. It's usually written in three stanzas of varying length. Like all lyric poems, odes are personal and full of strong feelings. The speaker in this poem LOVES soccer and its "lovely" soccer ball. What other details prove his love?

Ballad of My Bowling Ball

This year I asked on my birthday
For a sport to entertain.
And so my friends and I did go
To the local bowling lanes.

We laughed, we joked, we put on shoes.
My friends each picked a ball.
But I moaned in fright when I saw what was left—
The most enormous ball of all!

TELLING TALES

26

A **ballad** tells a story, usually about a hero or a memorable event. It often contains action, dialogue, and a rhyming pattern.

Long ago, ballads weren't written down. They were often sung. Read this poem aloud, and try turning it into a song!

It must have weighed 500 pounds.
And oh, that ball did shine!
With both my hands I strained to lift
Then let it drop—BONK!—at the line.

Ten pins stood silent at the end of the lane.
A strike! Yes, that was my goal.
After the drop, I began to grin,
For my ball was starting to roll!

Faster it rolled toward the 10 silent pins,
Like the lane was slicked with butter.
Yes, it's rolling straight! Oh ... but now it ain't ...
Oh drat, my ball's in the gutter.

—Mark Weakland

PRACTICE IT! ●

Starting to understand the tools poets use? There are lots of them! The following questions will help you practice with a few tools first before you sit down to write. (Hint: Find a word you don't understand? Look in the Glossary on page 30.)

• When words end in the same sound, they rhyme, such as in the poem "Ode to Quarterback Joe" on pages 12 and 13. Find other poems in this book that have rhyming lines. Do the rhymes always appear in a pattern?

• The poem "Barnyard Soccer" (page 22) introduced you to alliteration. Find at least three other poems that use alliteration.

• In "Cross-Country Runners" (page 8), the poet separates groups of lines and ideas with stanzas. Find other poems that use stanzas.

• "Ping-Pong" (page 20) is a free verse poem—it doesn't use a pattern of rhyming words or rhythms. Find another example of free verse in this book.

• You can get a good picture of a poem because of imagery. Which poems created good pictures in your mind? What were some of the details in those poems?

• When poets use **personification**, they give human movements, feelings, and interests to non-human things. For example, real hippos don't play hockey. But in "Animal Games" (page 19), they do. A zebra even plays Frisbee with a chimp! Find another poem that uses personification.

WRITE IT!

Here's an activity that will help you discover the poet in you!

GO SCOUTING

Find a sporting event. Live is best, but a game on TV or the Internet will work too. Check out a soccer game or a horse race. Visit a tennis court, hockey rink, or baseball diamond.

1) GET A PEN AND A NOTEBOOK.

2) START WATCHING.

Pay close attention to everything around you, and take notes. Describe the action. Use all your senses: sight, hearing, smell, touch, and taste. Stop once in a while and close your eyes. Doing so may help you hear or smell things more clearly.

3) PICK SOMETHING YOU'D LIKE TO WRITE ABOUT.

Let's say you pick a specific basketball player. Watch him or her for awhile, and make of list of everything you notice.

- What does he or she look like? What colors are on his or her uniform, and what do those colors remind you of? Describe the player's size and shape. How does he or she move and act toward other players? What sounds does he or she make? Try comparing the player to something else, such as a type of animal or machine.

4) WHEN YOU'RE DONE, READ THROUGH YOUR LIST.

Choose three things you really like—things you can see and remember clearly. Then try writing a poem about the basketball player. Start with a shorter poem first—a haiku, for example, rather than a ballad—until you get used to writing. Use the poems from the book as examples. "Old Manny" (page 10) might be useful if you're writing a limerick. If you want to write an acrostic, check out "Baseball" (page 9).

GLOSSARY ●

acrostic—a poem that uses the first letters of each line to spell out a word, name, or phrase relating to the poem's topic

alliteration—the use of two or more words that start with the same letter sound

ballad—a rhythmic poem that tells a story and is often sung

beat—a stressed word or syllable in a line of poetry

cinquain—a five-line poem that follows a 2-4-6-8-2 pattern of syllables

concrete poem—a poem that takes the shape of its subject

couplet—a pair of rhyming lines that usually have the same number of beats; couplets make their own point, create a separate image, or summarize the idea of a poem

dialogue—the words spoken between two or more characters (people or creatures); in writing, dialogue is set off with quotation marks

diamante—a seven-line poem that forms a diamond shape and follows this pattern: 1 noun, 2 adjectives, 3 verbs, 4 nouns, 3 verbs, 2 adjectives, 1 noun

free verse—a poem that follows no set rhythm or meter

haiku—a three-line poem that follows a 5-7-5 pattern of syllables

imagery—language that creates pictures in a reader's mind

limerick—a silly five-line poem in which the first two lines rhyme with the last, and the third and fourth lines rhyme with each other

lyric poem—a poem that expresses strong, personal feelings; sonnets, odes, and elegies are examples of lyric poetry

metaphor—a figure of speech that compares different things without using words such as "like" or "as"

meter—the pattern of beats in each line of a poem

narrative poem—a poem that tells a story

ode—a type of lyric poem, usually written in three stanzas with varying line lengths

personification—giving human characteristics, or traits, to something that isn't human

quatrain—a four-line group of poetry

repetition—saying something again and again

rhyme—word endings that sound the same

rhythm—a pattern of beats, like in music

simile—a figure of speech that compares different things by using the words "like" or "as"

sonnet—a poem that has 14 lines and a fixed pattern of rhymes

stanza—a grouping of lines in poetry

stanza break—the blank line that separates stanzas

syllable—a unit of sound in a word

READ MORE

Fandel, Jennifer. *You Can Write Cool Poems. You Can Write.* North Mankato, Minn.: Capstone Press, 2012.

Florian, Douglas. *Poem Runs: Baseball Poems and Paintings.* Boston: Harcourt Children's Books, 2012.

Low, Alice. *The Fastest Game on Two Feet.* New York: Holiday House, 2009.

Prelutsky, Jack. *Pizza, Pigs, and Poetry: How to Write a Poem.* New York: Greenwillow Books, 2008.

Salas, Laura Purdie. *Picture Yourself Writing Poetry: Using Photos to Inspire Writing. See It, Write It.* Mankato, Minn.: Capstone Press, 2012.

LOOK FOR ALL THE BOOKS IN THE SERIES:

PUCKS, CLUBS, AND BASEBALL GLOVES:
READING AND WRITING SPORTS POEMS

THORNS, HORNS, AND CRESCENT MOONS:
READING AND WRITING NATURE POEMS

TICKLES, PICKLES, AND FLOOFING PERSNICKLES:
READING AND WRITING NONSENSE POEMS

TRUST, TRUTH, AND RIDICULOUS GOOFS:
READING AND WRITING FRIENDSHIP POEMS

INTERNET SITES

FactHound offers a safe, fun way to find Internet sites related to this book. All of the sites on FactHound have been researched by our staff.

Here's all you do:
Visit www.facthound.com
Type in this code: 9781479521968

Super-cool stuff! Check out projects, games and lots more at **www.capstonekids.com**